FEDERICO E. TURK

GW00759847

STATISTICS
without
EQUATIONS

In collaboration with MATTIA VERONESE

Printed by CreateSpace
Published independently
Graphics and design by Federico Baratto
London, 2016

To Betta, Filippo and Teresa

TABLE OF
CONTENTS

PREFACE

This book is mainly concerned with the introduction, to the widest possible audience, of the basic concepts behind statistics. Statistics is a very important tool for the use of quantitative data that, in this digital era of ours, permeate all fields, from education to science and businesses of any kind.

Advances in digital processing allow the collection and manipulation of huge amount of data (the so called "Big Data") and have provided us with computer software and analytical packages that enable the application of sophisticated statistical analyses and tests without the need of a detailed understanding of the mathematics.

The ensuing freedom from complicated calculations enables us to have more focus on the concepts and ideas behind the use of statistics and, hopefully, it will also expand the number of users.

Hence in this book the reader will not find formulas but attempts to understand and visualize the process of statistical modelling and testing.

I sincerely hope that this attempt will be helpful to some.

London, January 2nd, 2015

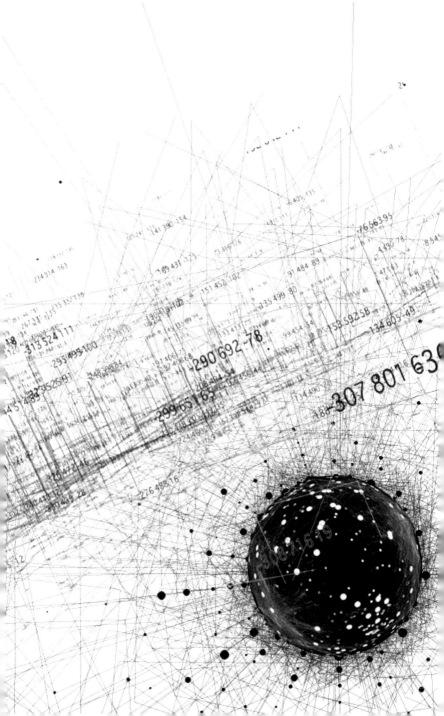

1 STATISTICS
MAKING INFERENCES
IN THE DIGITAL WORLD

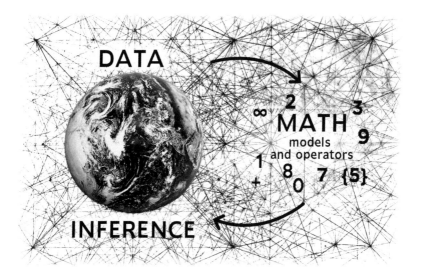

The one incontrovertible fact of modern societies is that information is produced, transmitted and used in digital form. Whether it is a piece of software, text, an image or a photo or a painting, a piece of music or a video, a payment, even a personal quip or a like or dislike on a social site, everything or almost everything now is produced transmitted and stored as a set of numbers.

The digitalization of the world has one important, although not always appreciated, consequence. Numbers can be easily stored, organized and then inserted into mathematical models with the aim of extracting patterns, quantifying relationships and, ultimately, predicting future events.

This endeavour is obviously not new. The painstakingly accurate observations of Tycho Brahe in the XVIth century were used by Kepler to discover the elliptical orbits of the planets. What is new though is the pervasiveness of numbers in modern society and in the sciences.

Mathematical models are now used to predict customer spending, direct police activity towards areas where future crime is likely, produce accurate weather forecasts, trade stocks and assets on financial markets, calculate cost of insurance policies, automatically control airplanes ships and motor vehicles etc.

Importantly, math is now permeating the experimental process in the biological and medical sciences. Here the decisional process is now driven by quantitative inferences, e.g. decisions based on the output of models that use numerical observations processed through mathematical models.

MATHEMATICS .... BUT WHY STATISTICS?

Having made the case for mathematics we have however not made the most important case, the case for statistics. We know mathematics can explain relations amongst data so why is there a need for statistics and, more importantly, what is statistics?

Look here on the right. For each value of a variable X we have collected a value for the variable Y. Note that the relationship between X and Y can be explained by a mathematical model, a line. Note also that for every value of X the correspondent Y is perfectly specified. The model therefore expresses a "deterministic" relationship between the two variables.

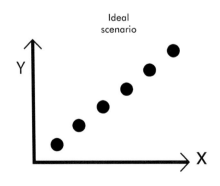

Ideal scenario

Now we move to a more realistic scenario. The measured relationship between Y and X is depicted on the right. Although there seems to be still some sort of linear relationship between X and Y, the linear dependency does not predict entirely the variation in Y. Indeed we can decompose the relation in the sum of two components.

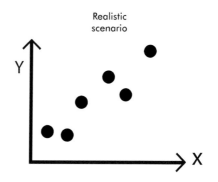

Realistic scenario

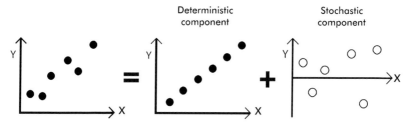

Deterministic component

Stochastic component

The first component is deterministic and establishes a mathematical relationship between X and Y, a line. The second component is the difference between the original data and the line, hence some of these numbers are positive and some are negative. It is clearly not deterministic and it actually looks very random. For this component we are unable to find a mathematical relationship that may predict Y from X. This is because it is not a deterministic component but a "stochastic" component that is dealt with by a very specific branch of mathematics which is called "statistics".

STOCHASTIC

To understand the meaning of stochastic we resort to the ancient Greeks who were the first to grasp the concept and invent a word (pronounce 'stokos') to describe it. The word means "target" but also "conjecture" as these two meanings coupled together express a process that is very much like hitting a practice target with a thrust weapon as the result is not always deterministic but has some uncertainty. Let's then use this same example, e.g. hitting a target, to gain some intuition on how stochastic processes emerge.

Στόχος - Stokos

Let's imagine that our ancient Greek warrior is hitting a target that looks like the one aside. For sake of simplicity we will record the result of each hit with a number corresponding to the colour. We also assume that in hitting the target, the warrior wishes to hit the target from the outside to the inside in the sequence 5, 6,…,10 and then from the inside to the outside.

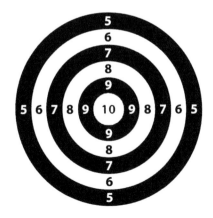

We shall start with the first experiment whereas the warrior is really close to the target:

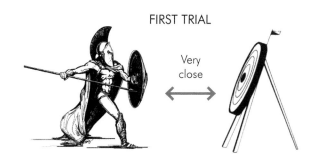

FIRST TRIAL

Very close

First result: 5,6,7,8,9,10,9,8,7,6,5

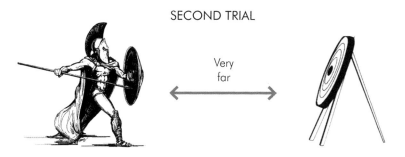

SECOND TRIAL

Very far

Second result: 6,9,5,10,6,8,7,6,8,5,9

The first sequence is a deterministic sequence. The second sequence is random, why? Because by placing the target very far we have lost control of the outcome of the process. In the first trial we can exactly predict what number will follow each, in the second trial we have no certain way to determine the outcome that can only be predicted using a new concept, probability.

Statistics is the branch of mathematics that deals with processes that are not deterministic but stochastic.

Natural processes are commonly "stochastic" in nature. By this we mean that the measurements we obtain vary and that this variation cannot be entirely controlled or explained in a deterministic fashion.

Understanding the stochastic properties of a measurement is therefore an important part of the scientific process and statistics is the science that takes care of this task.

2 THE PROCESS OF SCIENTIFIC INFERENCE

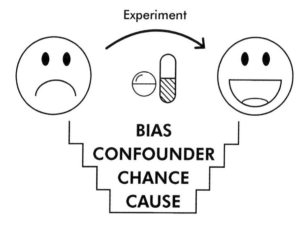

Experiment

BIAS
CONFOUNDER
CHANCE
CAUSE

Let's now consider the scientific process. One considers a certain exposure (a disease, a drug, an experimental manipulation), makes some measurements and, hopefully, will observe a change (e.g. an association). Is this association true? There are only four possible explanations for an observed association: experimental bias, the presence of a confounder, stochastic variation and a true causal association. The job of a scientist is to design an experiment and use statistical methodology to devise a bias free experiment, to control for the effect of a confounder and finally to assess the amount of stochastic variation in order to confirm a true cause-effect association.

BIAS

Bias is a systematic error. Bias has three sources:

1. *the observer/experimenter*
2. *the responder/experimental subject*
3. *the subject selection process.*

OBSERVER BIAS:

Observer bias occurs when the researcher who knows the goals of the study and/or the gene-rating hypotheses allows this knowledge to in-fluence the observations during the study.

Observer bias can be removed by "blinding", meaning that the appropriate precautions will be taken so that the researcher will have no way of knowing which subjects are taking the intervention and which ones are not. Blinding is removed when the data collection is completed. To ensure bias-free, the analysis may be under-taken by another independent researcher under a pre-defined analysis plan.

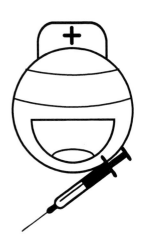

RESPONDER BIAS:

Responder bias occurs when the subject of the experiment who knows the goals of the study allows this knowledge to influence his/her response to the study intervention.

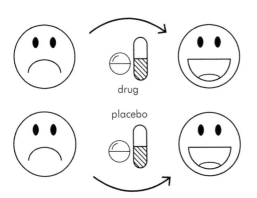

drug

placebo

PLACEBO

A placebo is a simulated or medically ineffective tre-atment intended to deceive the recipient.

Sometimes patients given a placebo treatment will have a perceived or actual improvement in a medical condition, a phenomenon commonly called the place-bo effect.

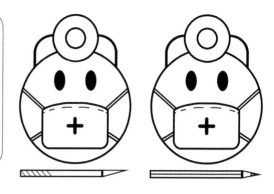

To avoid responder bias, sometimes it is necessary to use some form of deception, such as inert tablets (placebo), the infusion of inert vehicles, or sham interventions such as sham surgery, sham electrodes etc.

FURTHER READING:

Beecher, H. K. (1955). "The powerful placebo". Journal of the American Medical Association 159 (17): 1602–1606

Hróbjartsson A, Gøtzsche PC (20 January 2010). "Placebo interventions for all clinical conditions". In Hróbjartsson, Asbjørn. Cochrane Database Syst Rev 106 (1): CD003974

SELECTION BIAS – THE HIERARCHY OF EXPERIMENTAL DESIGNS

The way one chooses the subjects of the experiment is key to the avoidance of unwanted bias in the observations. An experiment requires the selection of a group of subjects to which the treatment is applied as well as a group of controls that provides the baseline. Below are the main different approaches to create the groups organized hierarchically.

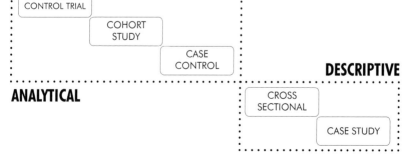

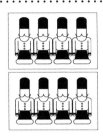

TREATMENT

RANDOMIZATION

NO
TREATMENT

RANDOMIZED CONTROL TRIAL

The randomised controlled trial is the most rigorous way of eliminating bias from an experimental setting. It has several important features:

• Patients are randomly allocated to intervention groups
• Patients and researchers are both blinded and remain unaware of which treatment was given until the study is completed.
• All groups are handled identically except for the experimental treatment

The randomization step makes sure that the unwanted effect of any factor that may affect the outcome is neutralized as it is dispersed randomly in the two groups.

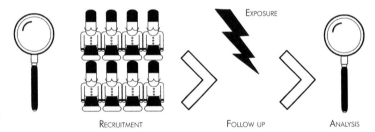

EXPOSURE

RECRUITMENT   FOLLOW UP   ANALYSIS

COHORT STUDY

In a prospective cohort study, the experimenter selects a group of subjects and then follows them up longitudinally. The assumption of this design is that during the follow-up period there will be some exposure of the subjects to factors of interest and that the researcher will be able to evaluate the cause-effect chain by being in tight control of the setting.

In a retrospective cohort study, the subjects are selected at the end. The experimental control of the follow-up period can only be exerted by looking into medical notes and include or exclude subjects according to the parameters set out by the experimenter. The retrospective design is not as rigorous as the prospective but obviously cheaper and quicker. It is also more appropriate in the case of rare diseases or exposures.

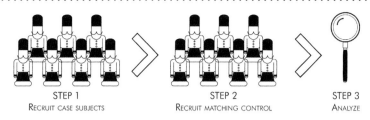

STEP 1
RECRUIT CASE SUBJECTS

STEP 2
RECRUIT MATCHING CONTROL

STEP 3
ANALYZE

CASE - CONTROL STUDY

The case-control study is a very common experimental paradigm. The experimenter first selects the population of interest and, afterwards, tries to find a control population that matches all the features of the experimental subjects except for the parameter that is the focus of the research question. This parameter can be a disease, an exposure etc. The process of matching is, however, arduous and the elimination of selection bias is far from guaranteed.

CROSS-SECTIONAL STUDY

A cross-sectional study is an observational study where a population is observed to assess the prevalence of a certain disease or condition and to explore possible cause-effect relationships that can be then analysed with better analytical designs. It is commonly used in epidemiology.

SINGLE-CASE STUDY

The single-case study is a descriptive or exploratory analysis of a single person, group or event that is aimed at unearthing a cause-effect relationship. The case-study report of a cluster of Kaposi's Sarcoma and Pneumocystis carinii Pneumonia in California in 1981 sparked the first investigation into AIDS.

CHANCE

This is the step when one quantifies the stochastic component in an experiment. It consists in the following steps.

1. Selection of a specific measure or end-point.
2. Quantification of the variability of this end-point.
3. Testing of whether the change in end-point is likely to be stochastic or deterministic.

END POINT:

Smileys size

VARIABILITY:

Normal smileys size

TEST:

Is this one smiley different
from the norm?

CONFOUNDER

In statistics, a confounding variable (also confounder) is an extraneous variable that is associated with both the exposure and the outcome. Hence, the observed exposure-outcome relation is a spurious one as both are instead driven by the confounder.

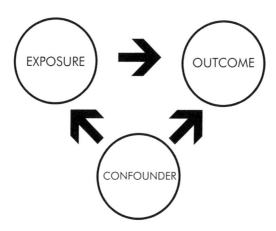

As an example, suppose that a relation is observed between caffeine consumption and heart disease.

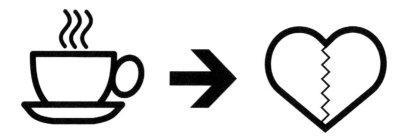

The observation is a compelling one and one may start thinking that coffee is a possible cause of cardiac disorders.
However there may be a hidden confounder that creates this relation as spurious.

In this case the spurious variable is smoking. Those who smoke have higher caffeine intake and also higher risk of heart disease. Heart disease therefore is not due to caffeine. The existence of confounders is a big threat to scientific inference. Depending on the study design, strategies can be adopted to avoid confounding effects on outcomes.

RANDOMIZATION
The simple action of randomizing a group of subjects towards exposure (say subjects are randomly assigned to two groups, one with high coffee consumption and one will low one) is able to eliminate the bias introduced by the confounder.

EXPERIMENTATION
In Case-Control design, the two groups should be matched for the value or range of the confounder.

STRATIFICATION
In cohort studies, subjects may be divided in sub-groups with different values of the confounder. For example, the association between caffeine and heart risk can be evaluated in a number of sub-groups with different smoking habits. If the association changes from group to group then the confounding effect is likely.

REGRESSION
If none of the above is possible, one can simply record the values of the confounder in each subject and then introduce them in the final analysis. Note, however, that this should be a method of last resort and is not as effective as the ones defined above.

CAUSE

Once the effects of bias, chance and confounders have been ruled out, one can turn to inferring the cause-effect relationship. This is the core aim of the scientific method but is not automatic. The "Discussion" section of a scientific paper is the one devoted to this particular task that has been codified in 1965 by Sir Austin Bradford Hill.

In this framework, judgement of a cause-effect relationship is based on a chain of logical factors that addresses two main areas:

- Observed association between an exposure and a disease is valid.

- Totality of evidence from a number of sources supports a judgement of causality.

BRADFORD-HILL CRITERIA

1. STRENGTH
The stronger the association between exposure and disease the more likely that it is causal.

2. CONSISTENCY
The relationship is likely to be causal if the association has been replicated.

3. SPECIFICITY
The more specific an association is between an exposure and a disease the more likely there is causal relationship between the two.

4. TEMPORAL RELATIONSHIP
The closer in time the association the more likely to be causal (with disease following exposure obviously).

5. DOSE-RESPONSE RELATIONSHIP
If increasing levels of exposure lead to increasing risks of disease the association is likely causal.

6. PLAUSIBILITY
A plausible mechanism between cause and effect increases the likelihood of causality.

7. COHERENCE
Coherence implies that a cause and effect interpretation does not conflict with what is known of the natural world.

8. EXPERIMENTAL EVIDENCE
There is a consistent association in animal and human experiments.

9. ANALOGY
One draws strength from the effects between similar factors.

PROBABILITIES
AND
3 PROBABILITY
CALCULUS

As noted in the previous chapter, the role of statistics is to "rule out" that a certain finding is not due to chance, in other words is to quantify the stochastic component of a measurement.

Hence we first need to define stochastic processes in order to understand what is stochastic and what is not. A stochastic process is defined by a probability function.

Probability is the relative occurrence of a random event in an infinite (or very large) number of trials.

We can use two stochastic types of events to help us understand a few important concepts in probabilities. We use the toss of a coin and the throw of a dice. These are both stochastic as their outcome cannot be predicted with certainty.

EXPERIMENT	TOSSING A COIN	THROWING A DICE
Sample space	Head, Tail	1, 2, 3, 4, 5, 6
Sample point	Either head or tail	Either 1 or 2 or 3 or 4 or...
Event/Outcome	The outcome of n tosses	The outcome of n throws
Probability	1/2 for each sample point	1/6 for each sample point

While the probability of a single sample point may be easy and intuitive to understand, the probability of more complex outcomes may be a bit more difficult to obtain and/or understand. For example what is the probability of having two heads and one tail? Is that different from the probability of having the outcome {tail, tail, head}? What is the probability of the outcome {2, 3, 5, 2, 1} out of five throws? In order to progress our understanding of probabilities we need to learn three fundamental properties.

MUTUALLY EXCLUSIVE EVENTS AND THE SUM PRINCIPLE

Two events A and B are **mutually *exclusive*** if the occurrence of one excludes the occurrence of the other.

Let's take the example of cards taken out of a deck. Two events defined as the "extraction of a King" and "the extraction of an Ace" are mutually exclusive because if one takes place the other can't. However two events such as "the extraction of Kings" and "the extraction of Hearts" are not mutually exclusive because one card can be a King and a Heart at the same time.

If two events, A and B, are mutually exclusive, the probability of occurrence of the event **A or B** is the sum of the two probabilities.

EXAMPLE:

The throw of a dice implies 6 events that are mutually exclusive, each with probability 1/6. What is the probability of an even outcome? The probability of the outcome being even (2 or 4 or 6) is the sum of the individual probabilities 3/6=0.5.

MUTUALLY CONDITIONAL EVENTS AND THE PRODUCT PRINCIPLE

Two outcomes A and B are **mutually *conditional*** if the occurrence of A depends on the occurrence of B or vice versa.

Let's look again at the example of cards taken out of a deck. Consider two sequential events defined as the "extraction of a first card" and "the extraction of a second card". If the card taken out first is not placed back into the deck, the second event is conditional on the first as there will be one less card in the deck which will change the probabilities of the second event.

If the event B is conditional on the event A, the probability of occurrence of the event **A and B** is the product of the probability of A times the probability of B given A.

EXAMPLE:

Suppose that two cards are extracted (but not replaced) from the same deck. What is the probability of extracting 2 hearts? The probability of extracting a heart at the first step is 13/52 (all cards equally likely). The probability of a second heart taken out is (13-1)/(52-1). The probability of two hearts being extracted is the product of the two probabilities = 0.0588.

INDEPENDENT EVENTS
AND THE PRODUCT PRINCIPLE

Two outcomes A and B are **independent** if the occurrence of A does not depend on the occurrence of B and vice versa.

In example of cards taken out of a deck we still consider the two sequential events defined as the "extraction of a first card" and "the extraction of a second card". If the card taken out first is now placed back into the deck the two events are independent. This time the probabilities of the second event are not conditioned by what happened during the first extraction.

If the event A and event B are independent, the probability of occurrence of the event **A and B** is the product of the probability of A times the probability of B.

EXAMPLE:

Suppose that two cards are extracted (and then replaced) from the same deck. What is the probability of extracting 2 hearts? The probability of the second card is now independent from the card extracted first. The probability of extraction of two hearts is now simply the square of the probability of extraction of one heart = $(13/52)^2 = 0.0625$.

WORKING OUT PROBABILITIES
WITH PROBABILISTIC TREES

Probabilistic trees or tree diagrams are graphical tools that allow to visualize all the outcomes of an event and to calculate the relative probabilities.
Let's demonstrate one of these trees using the standard coin toss. First of all we lay out the series of events. In this case we assume two sequential tosses. Then we lay on the relative probabilities.

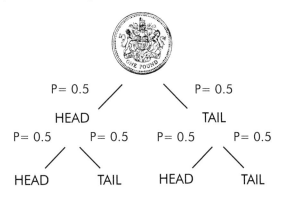

The problem is now on how do we use the tree to calculate probabilities. The way to go about is to calculate the probabilities of each of the series of outcomes by multiplying the probabilities met across the path.

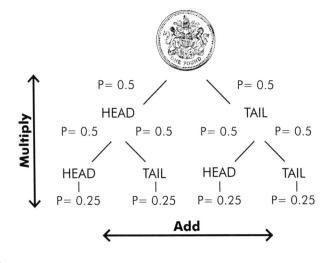

The probability of two Heads (or two Tails) is therefore 0.5*0.5 =0.25. But what about the probability of obtaining one head and one tail? This can happen when either the final outcome is one head first and then one tail (probability =0.5*0.5=0.25) but also by having one tail first and then one head (again probability = 0.5*0.5 = 0.25). The probability of having either a head and tail or a tail and a head as we learnt before is obtained by adding the two probabilities (0.25+0.25=0.5).

EXAMPLE:

There are two bags, bag A and bag B. Bag A contains 3 blue marbles and 4 red marbles. Bag B contains 5 blue marbles and 3 red marbles. You take one marble from bag A and one marble from bag B. What is the probability of you taking 1 red and 1 blue marble?

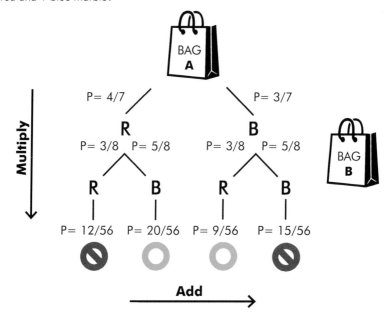

We build the tree above that depicts the sequence of drawings from the two bags. Note that in this case the exact sequence (Bag A before or after Bag B) is not relevant but that the tree could handle more complex cases as well. The probability can be calculated by summing the probabilities of the two sequences Red and Blue plus Blue and Red that are signed with the green post. The total probability is 20/56+9/56 = 29/56.

CONDITIONAL PROBABILITIES AND THE BAYES THEOREM

It is very common to encounter in sciences or daily life the need to calculate the conditional probability of two events that are not independent. This calculation, first introduced by reverend Thomas Bayes, states the following:

"If A and B are two events, the probability of A conditional to B being true is equal to the probability of A divided by the probability of B times the probability of B if A is true."

This is a very important theorem as it allows to work out probabilities of events that are dependent from each other which is a paramount activity in any job that involves the use of logic (e.g. if you are a doctor, a lawyer, Sherlock Holmes etc.). However it is also difficult to apply and unintuitive. Here we show two similar approaches for its solution, one using probabilistic trees and one using natural probabilities. We will illustrate the methods using two examples.

EXAMPLE 1:

In a school 60% of the students are boys and 40% are girls. All boys wear trousers, 50% of girls wear trousers. An observer sees a student wearing trousers, what is the probability that it is a girl?

SOLUTION USING A PROBABILISTIC TREE

*The probabilistic tree below allows the application of Bayes theorem. The probabi-
lity we are looking for is the probability that someone wearing trousers is a girl. The
probability of someone wearing trousers being a girl is equal to the probability of
students being girls (0.4) divided by the probability of someone wearing trousers
(0.2+0.6=0.8) times the probability of girls wearing trousers (0.5). The final calculation (0.4*0.5/0.8 = 0.25) produces the required answer.*

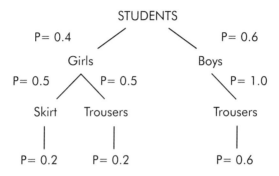

SOLUTION USING THE NATURAL PROBABILITIES APPROACH

*We start solving the problem assuming that the school has 1000 students (1000 is
a good number to use). The problem above becomes the following. A school has
1000 students of which 600 are boys, 400 are girls. 200 girls wear trousers. What
percentage of those wearing trousers are girls?*
*The answer is that of the total 800 students, boys and girls, wearing trousers, 200
are girls.Hence the probability is equal to 200/800=0.25.*

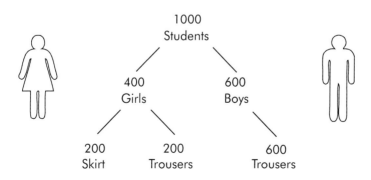

EXAMPLE 2:

Before going away for a month, you ask one of your friends to fee your water-turtle. Without food, the turtle has a 80 percent chance of dying. But even with proper feeding it still has a 10 percent chance of dying. The probability that your friend will forget to feed the turtle is 20 percent. (a) What's the chance that your turtle will survive the month? (b) If it's dead when you return, what's the chance that your friend forgot to feed it?

SOLUTION USING A PROBABILISTIC TREE

The application of the Bayes theorem can be visualized as follows.

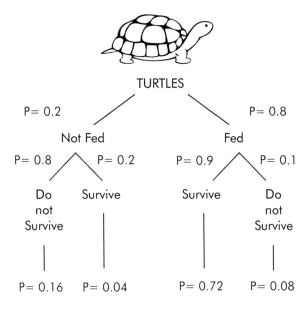

The first answer can be readily worked out by being the sum of 0.72 plus 0.04 = 0.76.

For the second answer, the probability we are looking for is the probability that our friend did not feed the turtle if the turtle turns out to be dead. This is equal to the probability that the turtle was not fed (0.2) divided by the probability of the turtle dying (0.08+0.16=0.24) times the probability of not surviving because not fed (0.8). The total (0.2*0.8/0.24)=0.66.

SOLUTION USING THE NATURAL PROBABILITIES APPROACH

We start assuming a good number of turtles, this time say 100. Then the problem can be visualized as follows.

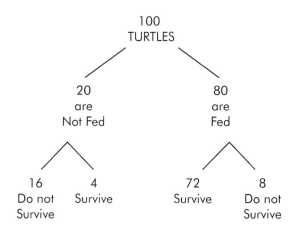

To answer question a) we note that out of the 100 turtles, out of all the possible scenarios 72+4 will survive. Hence the probability is 76/100 = 0.76

To answer question b) we note that 16 will be the ones dying if not fed by your friend out of a total of 16+8 turtles that die. Hence the probability that, if dead, it was your friend's fault is 16/(16+8) = 2/3.

4 PROBABILITY DISTRIBUTIONS

In order to know that a result is NOT due to a stochastic process is key to define what a stochastic process actually IS. Hence we need to construct probability distributions for the most common stochastic processes we are going to encounter. We start with the probability distribution of a purely stochastic process that has only two possible outcomes.

THE BINOMIAL DISTRIBUTION

The binomial distribution is the discrete probability distribution of the number of successes in a sequence of n independent yes/no experiments, each of which yields success with a fixed probability. We build a probabilistic tree that is now a bit different and we call it a binomial tree. The tree looks like this:

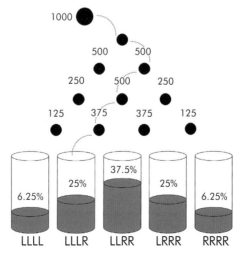

This time, out of each node, on the level below we do not have two more nodes as two shared nodes are collapsed into one. In the example above, a ball can either go left (L) or right (R), in this instance with the same probability 0.5. This is a binomial event and is modelled by a binomial distribution. We can use the binomial distribution to calculate the probability that the ball has gone 3 times left and one right.

Because the order by which the events happen is not relevant in the binomial distribution, the middle nodes can be collapsed into one. For example, the probabilities of a ball going left and right is not qualified in terms of what happened first. So, on the second row, the L and R and the R and L sequences are collapsed into one. The probability can then be calculated as usual, in this case using a natural probability approach starting with 1000 balls and working out where they are going to end up.

The scheme above can be used to derive binomial probabilities. For example, what is the probability of having 4 subsequent tails when tossing a coin? If we take "ball bouncing left" as the "tail" event and "ball bouncing right" as the "head" event than 6.25% is the probability. On the other hand 25% is the probability of having 3 tails and one head out of 4 tosses and so forth.

Hence, the tree above can be used to check whether one particular event can be attributed to a binomial distribution with a certain probability.

So, if one wants to know whether a coin is perfectly balanced, all it has to do is to flip it for a certain amount of times (the more the better). Now suppose that the coin has been flipped 10 times and has produced a sequence of 10 tails. How likely is that coin to be coming from a binomial distribution with a 0.5 probability? Well the probability of such a sequence having come from a binomial distribution with 0.5 probability is very small 0.001, so the likelihood of that coin being balanced is also small.

EXAMPLE:

Suppose that the percentage of smokers in the general population is p=0.30. I take a sample of 5 subjects from a certain group and 4 of them are smokers. What is the probability that this group belongs to the normal population?

We can use the binomial tree with probability 0.3 for one event and 0.7 for the opposite. The tree is shown below. This can then be generalized to the probability of extracting from the general population 4 smokers out of 5 subjects. The probability is 29/1000 =0.029 which is very low. This means that the group where I took my sample from is unlikely to belong to the general population because their smoking habits are different. Indeed in the population where I took my random sample from, people seem to smoke more than one would expect.

GENERAL POPULATION

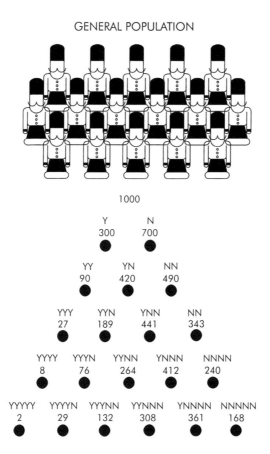

THE CENTRAL LIMIT THEOREM AND THE GAUSSIAN DISTRIBUTION

The Gaussian or "Normal" distribution is the probability distribution of a stochastic variable that is continuous, e.g. can take any real value. In experimental sciences it is used as the paradigmatic distribution for stochastic processes. The reason why this distribution, and not others or many others distributions, are used stands in its usefulness and general validity which is defined by the Central Limit Theorem. Below is a visual representation of what this theorem says:

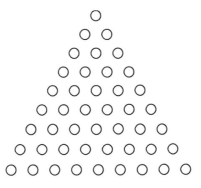

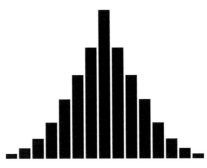

A continuous stochastic process may be represented by the output of a system made of a ball going through *N* subsequent layers that randomly divert its direction. In this model, each layer represents a single physical event that shifts the measurement either way. The whole measurement is then affected equally by a large number of these physical events that shift, by approximately the same amount, the measurement. As these physical elements of the system cannot be controlled, they ultimately generate a symmetric stochastic distribution. If the number N of these physical events is infinite, the distribution converges to the smooth, bell shaped curve called Gaussian distribution.

To demonstrate this concept differently, imagine that you are measuring the time a bus takes to go through its route from beginning to end. During its route the bus will stop at a number of bus-stops where it will have to collect a varying number of passengers. The bus will also go through a number of traffic-lights that will also delay its trip for an unpredictable amount of time. Seemingly unpredictable will also be the time the bus will take to go through turnabouts depending on traffic.

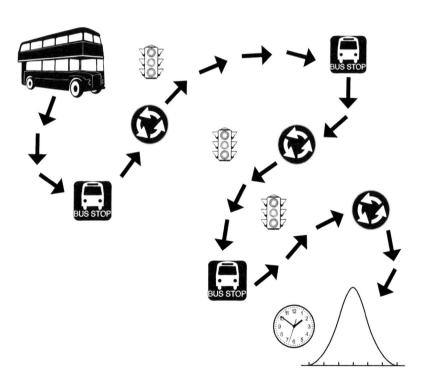

Each of the aforementioned physical events, that cannot be controlled and are therefore of stochastic nature, will shift the total travel time by a comparably similar amount of time backward and forward and the overall distribution of the recorded arrival time will result in being bell-shaped, symmetric and smooth.

The Gaussian or Normal distribution takes its name from Johann Carl Friedrich Gauss, a German mathematician and physicist who contributed significantly to number theory, algebra, analysis, statistics, astronomy, geophysics and optics.

Because the distribution is now continuous and smooth, the so called "buckets" that we used for the binomial distribution to calculate probabilities are no more. Besides, the value of the stochastic value X is now allowed to vary between plus and minus infinity.

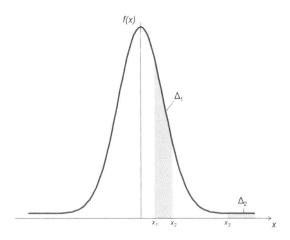

This means that, when we deal with continuous variables (e.g the time of the bus for its route), we can calculate probabilities only for intervals (say the intervals Δ_1 and Δ_2 above) as the corresponding area under the probability function ($f(x)$). In the figure above, Δ_1 is the probability of measurement X being in the interval $[x_1, x_2]$. Δ_2 instead is the probability of measurement X being greater than x_3.

OUTLIERS

The scheme above also allows us to introduce the concept of outliers. We suppose that one particular measurement was odd in that the bus was very late, far later than one would have expected from the distribution of the observations. This would be an outlier observation.

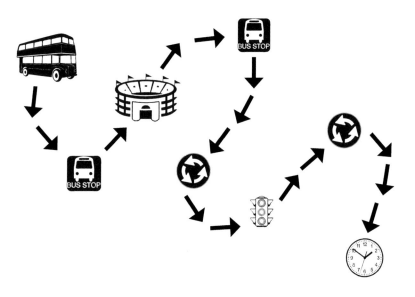

In this instance, the delay would be caused by an exceptional event whose effect is much larger than all the others put together. For example, the bus could have run while a football match had ended and could have got stuck in traffic for a very long time. The occurrence of football matches would therefore be factors that should be controlled for. Any experiment tried to speed up the bus and shorten the time it took to go through the route should have taken place strictly away from times of football matches.

In the more general context of scientific enquire, an outlier could represent either motivated mis-reporting, an error of data recording or entry, a malfunction of the measurement tool, or something more interesting. This extreme score might shed light on an important principle or issue. Before discarding outliers, researchers need to consider whether outliers signal that something is not right in the experimental setting and needs to be taken care of.

THE PARAMETERS
OF A
5 STOCHASTIC
PROCESS

The normal distribution is a fairly popular model for a continuous stochastic process that can be widely used in the physical and natural sciences. This is because we like to think that random variations in the data are produced by a very large number of sources that we cannot control, each deviating the number with a small effect; if in fact this is not the case and data contain many outliers, then we like to go back to the board and draw a better experiment. The normal distribution is depicted again below and is fully defined by two parameters:

Central Value: μ

Standard Deviation: σ (σ^2 is the variance)

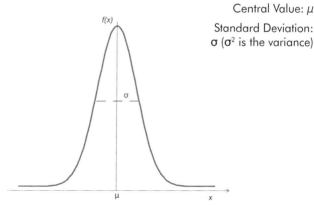

The central value is obviously the number around which the process develops and the standard deviation indicates how spread-out the stochastic process is. Although one only needs these two parameters to describe the stochastic process, these parameters are generally not known. However they can be estimated from the data.

The best numerical estimator that gets a value as close as possible to the real and unknown **μ** is the **arithmetic mean (or average)**. The arithmetic mean of a set of values is simply their sum divided by their number.

EXAMPLE:

One collects 5 values from a distribution with an unknown centre value μ and they are **1,2,3,4,5. What is the best estimate for the central value μ?**
The average is equal to the sum, **15**, divided by their number, **5**, and equals **3**.

The estimator for the variance **σ^2** of the distribution is the **sample variance**. This is equal to the s**um of the squared values, once the average has been subtracted from each of them, divided by the number of values minus 1**. The **sample standard deviation**, which is the estimator of the standard deviation **σ**, is the **squared root** of the sample variance.

EXAMPLE:

We now wish to estimate the unknown variance **σ^2** of the 5 values **1,2,3,4,5. What is the best estimate for the variance σ^2** and/or standard deviation **σ**?

We subtract the average **3** from each value and obtain -2, -1, 0, 1, 2. We then square them and take the sum. We obtain **4, 1, 0, 1, 4**. The sum is **10** that divided by **4** is then **2.5**. This is the sample variance. The sample standard deviation is its squared root, **1.58**.

OTHER ESTIMATORS – MEDIAN MID-RANGE

The mean or average is not the only estimator of the central value as the sample variance is not the only estimator or the variance. However these are the optimal estimators if the stochastic variable is normally distributed.

In those instances when the data are not normally distributed, e.g. when outlying observations are present, other estimators exist that perform better than the one above.

One commonly used estimator for the central value of a distribution is the **median**. Given a sequence of numbers the median is the number in the middle, the one that splits the sample in two. If there is an even number of observations, then there is no single middle value. The median is then usually defined to be the mean of the two middle values.

EXAMPLE:

One collects 5 values from a distribution with an unknown centre value μ and they are **1,2,3,4,5. What is the median if we wish to use it to estimate the central value μ?**
The median is 3.

EXAMPLE:

One collects 6 values from a distribution with an unknown centre value μ and they are **1,2,3,4,5,6. What is the median if we wish to use it to estimate the central value μ?**

In this case the middle value but we can average the two middle ones to get the median $(3+4)/2 = 3.5$.

The median may be an effective estimator when the sample contains outliers. Indeed, as long as extreme observations are rare, the median will be less swayed away than the mean.

EXAMPLE:

One collects 5 values from a distribution with an unknown centre value μ and they are 1,2,3,4,5. **Both the median and the mean are 3.**

We repeat the measurement and this time, unknown to us, the instrumentation malfunctions when the last value is acquired. Hence we obtain **1,2,3,4,10. The mean of the sample is 5 as the extreme observation sways it. The median instead is still 3.**

A similar estimator can be derived for the spread of the distribution that uses the properties of the median and is called the mid-range. The sample is first split in two by the median. The remaining two portions are again split in half by calculating the medians of the two half samples. The distance between the median of the upper half and the median of the lower half is the mid-range.

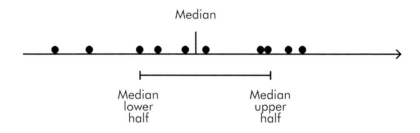

PLOTTING IT OUT – THE BOXPLOT

Although mean and sample variance are generally good to use with data, median and mid-range are particularly useful when one wishes to render graphically the sample.

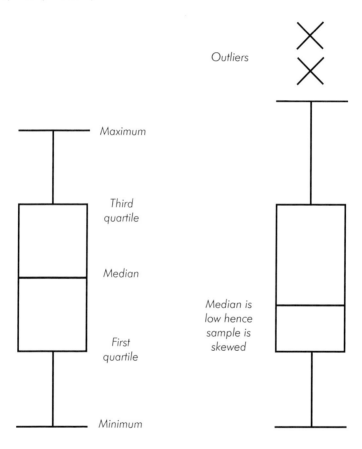

Outliers

Maximum

Third quartile

Median

First quartile

Minimum

Median is low hence sample is skewed

The use of box-plots, that display minimum, maximum, the inter-quartile range and, in case, show outliers, is preferable on top of any other display mode for samples (e.g. mean and standard deviation) as it fully displays the characteristics of the data.

6 MEASURING AND MEASURING AND MEASURING

It is worth now repeating that each measurement is made of a deterministic part (the one we are after) and a stochastic component. Now, the very important message of this chapter is that the variability of the stochastic component of a measurement can be reduced with a very simple trick: by repeating the measurement and taking averages. Hence, one can pick his/her own instrumentation and, as long as the measurable does not change for a while, repeat the measurement and take their average. The more the measurements, the less the variability of the average, the closer the average will be to the true value.

How is it possible that a very simple trick, such as repeating a measurement and taking an average, may reduce the variability of a random process? In order to explain that, let's make a simplifying assumption, that is that the measurement follows a Gaussian distribution.

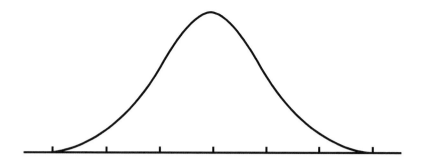

Let's now take a sequence of measurements that, for the sake of simplicity, have a central value of 0. In order to obtain an average, we have to add them up and then divide by their number. The first intuition we might have is that, by adding the measurement we are actually increasing the noise. This is actually true because:

NOTION 1: THE SUM OF N GAUSSIAN MEASUREMENTS HAS A VARIANCE WHICH IS EQUAL TO THE SUM OF THEIR VARIANCES

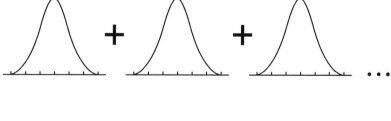

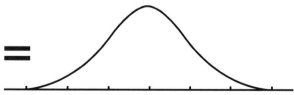

However, by taking an average we are just not summing but we are then diving by the number N of measurements. Now, if you divide by N a number its numerical variability will undoubtedly decrease. Indeed.

NOTION 2: A VARIABLE OBTAINED BY DIVIDING BY N A GAUSSIAN VARIABLE, HAS A STANDARD DEVIATION EQUAL TO 1/N OF THE ORIGINAL ONE (AND ITS VARIANCE IS 1/N² OF THE VARIANCE OF THE ORIGINAL VARIABLE).

Hence, the calculation of the average on one hand increases variance by a multiplicative factor of N but then it reduces by a factor $1/N^2$.

Hence the variance of the average of N measurements is 1/N the one of the single measurement (!!!)

This has enormous consequences because now we know that by repeating the measurement the resulting averages will get closer and closer to the real value.

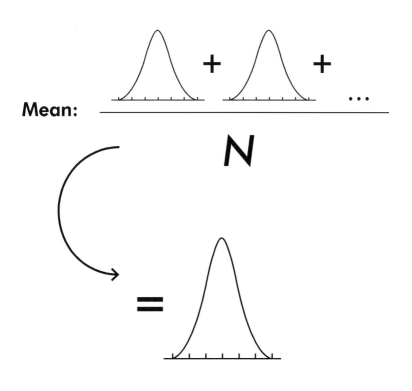

HOW BIG MUST BE *N*?
THE POWER CALCULATION

Statistical testing has one main purpose that was defined before. This purpose is to exclude that the observed effect is a mere effect of chance. Now we also know that we can reduce the stochastic/chance component with the simple trick of repeating the measurement. Of course in theory we could repeat a measurement thousands or millions of times so that the stochastic component will be reduced to 0. However this is generally not possible either because it is too impractical or simply too expensive. Hence, statistical testing must be preceded by an important step in the experimental design that is called power calculation.

The aim of power calculation is to calculate the sample size, that is the number *N* of samples required for your experiment.

The principle is illustrated below. Here we assume that we want to check whether two groups of people, say one set of volunteers taking a drug and another one taking a simple placebo, have different measurement, say blood pressure or something else. In order to design our experiment properly we have to:

1. Choose the measurement we want to do.

2. Take some preliminary measurements to ascertain the variability (the variance) of this measurement in the population.

3. Decide what is the MINIMAL EFFECT OF INTEREST. This is very important. Theoretically we could look for very small, tiny differences between the two groups but their value would be null. Hence we have to make-up our mind on what would be the value below which any observed difference would be meaningless.

4. Now there are two other parameters that are a bit less intuitive.

   a. **The TYPE I error**: this is the probability that the difference we will find, even passing the statistical test, will be a false positive. This might happen because stochastic processes are uncontrolled and there is always, really always, the risk of an extreme observation being picked up by chance. We want this probability to be small and traditionally is set to 0.05.

b. The POWER: this is the opposite. This is the probability of finding an effect if is really there. Again, the effect may be absconded by one extreme noise realization. We wish this probability to be high, say either 0.8 or 0.9.

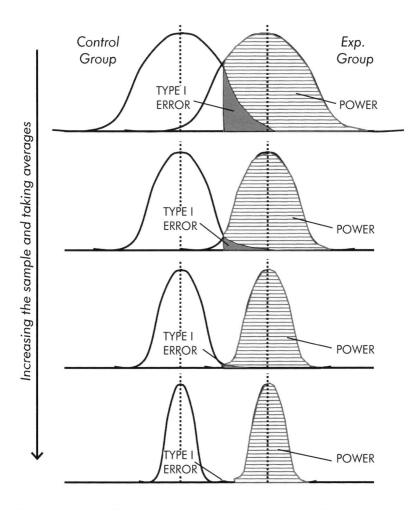

The graphs above illustrates how the distribution of the sample means of the two groups get tighter as the sample size increases. Seemingly the power of detection increases (dashes area) and the false positive rate (grey area) gets smaller.

7 RULING OUT CHANCE WITH HYPOTHESIS TESTING

The procedure by which we test whether the observed variation is stochastic or not is called Hypothesis Testing. We have seen examples before, but in a nutshell it consists in the following steps.

1. Encapsulate the observed variation into a statistic.

2. Compare the statistic with the distribution of the statistic under the Null Distribution.

3. The Null Distribution is the distribution of the statistic under the Null Hypothesis.

4. The Null Hypothesis is the hypothesis that the variation is only stochastic and due to uncontrolled variation.

5. If the statistic fits somewhere in the tails of the Null Distribution, then we can conclude that the variation is unlikely to be solely stochastic.

For example, suppose that, in some way which is not important here, we have sampled some data and calculated a statistic T. We know the distribution of that statistic under the Null Hypothesis.

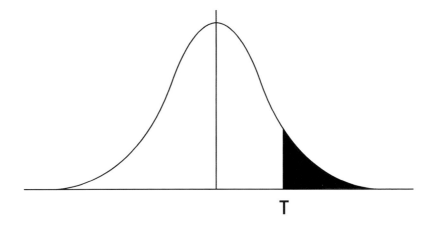

The statistic T looks quite extreme: one can calculate the p-value of this statistic which is the area under the tail of the distribution. If the p-value is small then it is very unlikely that the observed variation is stochastic. This is also called the 1-tail p-value because we assumed that the only reasonable non-stochastic effect would be positive. However we may not know in advance whether the change was positive or negative.

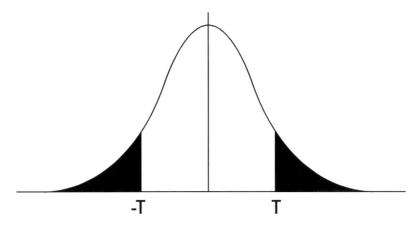

In this instance the p-value is equal to the area under the positive and negative tails (2 tails test).

DEGREES OF FREEDOM

We now start getting into the business of statistical testing and statistical testing requires the construction of statistics. As we have seen in the case of the sample mean, statistics can be obtained by combining measurements. All measurements are supposed to be independent from each other. Because they are independent, they are said to be "free" which means that can take any value according to the probability distribution. Every new independent measurement is said to add a degree of freedom. To give a sense of why this is the case, assume that three independent measurements X_1, X_2, X_3 are taken. Each has a numeric value. We can then imagine that these three numbers are the coordinates of a point P. Because there are three measurements, the point P is a point in a three-dimensional space.

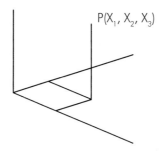

$P(X_1, X_2, X_3)$

As the coordinates X_1, X_2, X_3 are free to take any value, the point P has 3 degrees of freedom.

Adding independent measurements or creating averages create statistics that can also be defined as "free" to take values according to their distribution. As we have seen, in the case of the Gaussian distribution, summing or taking averages creates statistics that still follow the Gaussian distributions.

However when one calculates a statistic re-using the data things change. What does it mean to re-use the data? Consider the **way we calculate the sample standard deviation. We use the observations to calculate the sample mean first and then we re-use the same observations to calculate their squared deviation from the same mean**. Because we are re-using the same observations twice it is obvious that we are losing some information. **This concept is formally translated into the loss of one degree of freedom**.

This can be illustrated by the following example.

Using a computer, pairs of random numbers were drawn from a normal distribution. For every pair a point was drawn on the above plane. The first point that was generated was used as the X coordinate, the second point as the Y coordinate. By generating many pairs we were able to occupy the plane with a set of points.

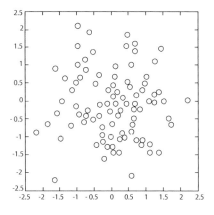

We then did the same thing with a twist: we again drew pairs of numbers from the same random generator. But this time, once we had the two numbers we a) calculated their average and b) calculated the difference of the two numbers from the average. It was these two numbers, the differences from the average, that we used as coordinates to draw the points on the 2-dimensional space.

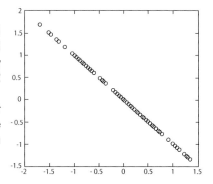

Although the numbers were still random, the points we draw did not cover the whole plain but oddly aligned on a line. From a space (2 degrees of freedom) to a line (1 degree of freedom).We have lost one degree of freedom because we have created a distribution of data re-using the sampled points.

The little experiment above mimics what is done when calculating standard deviations (calculate average and then calculate the root of sum of the squared difference of data from the average). In the same way we have lost a degree of freedom here, so we will lose one degree of freedom when we will calculate differences from an average. This happens all the time when we do statistical testing. So now when a statistical test asks or requires degrees of freedom you should know how to calculate them: number of data points you have used minus the times you have re-used them (generally 1).

CALCULATING PARAMETRIC STATISTICS

The statistic is a mathematical construct. The main aim behind the calculation of a statistic is that it has to be most sensitive to deviation from the Null Hypothesis. The second aim is that it has to be properly scaled so that its distribution is useful for any data.

The assumption behind the statistics we will be dealing with in this chapter is that stochastic variation in the measurement follows the Gaussian/Normal distribution. Hence these statistics are called parametric. This assumption is generally true for a number of experimental situations but not for all of them. If one does not know if the data are not normally distributed then he/she will have to use different statistics and tests that do not rely on this assumption. These statistics and tests are called non-parametric.

A parametric statistic is usually in either of the following forms:

T STATISTICS

$$T_{df} = Z/s$$

Z: A number sensitive to the alternative hypothesis (i.e., its magnitude tends to be large when the null hypothesis is false), usually is a difference (say between means) and has a sign.

s: A scaling factor that is usually calculated as the standard deviation of Z.

df: These are the degrees of freedom of s. As shown before is usually calculated as the number of data minus the number of means that are calculated from the data.

F STATISTICS

$$F_{df2}^{df1} = S/s$$

S: A number sensitive to the alternative hypothesis (i.e., its magnitude tends to be large when the null hypothesis is false), usually is a **squared** difference (say between data and their mean or between group means and a mean-of means). It doesn't have a sign. It is generally scaled to be comparable to s.

s: A scaling factor that is usually calculated as the standard deviation of the data.

df1: These are the degrees of freedom of S. It is usually calculated as the number of data (could be group means) minus the number of means that are calculated from the data.

df2: These are the degrees of freedom of s. It is usually calculated as the number of data minus the number of means that are calculated from the data.

TESTING A DIFFERENCE IN THE MEANS OF TWO GROUPS
(Student T Test - Independent Groups)

EXPERIMENT: You take samples from two groups that are independent and that you think differ by the level of a factor (a drug, a condition etc.).

STATISTIC: Student T statistic.

Z: Z is equal to the difference between the two sample means. This statistic may be positive or negative.

s: It is the standard deviation of Z. Note that Z is the difference between two means. Hence its variance is the sum of variances of the two means.

df: It is defined according to group variances.

Two Groups with Same Variance:
If the two groups have the same variance than an estimate of the variance itself can be easily calculated by pooling together the differences of all data from their respective means. Hence the *df* will be equal to the total number of data in the two groups minus the number of means, two.

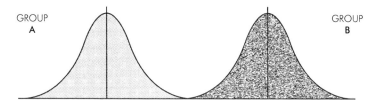

Two Groups with Different Variance:
If the two groups have the different variance than I need two estimate separately the variance of one group and the variance of the second group. In this case the *df* will be equal to mean of the *df* for the two groups.

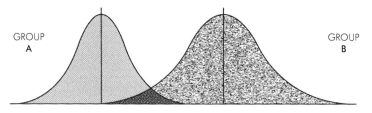

TESTING A DIFFERENCE IN THE MEANS OF THREE OR MORE GROUPS
(ANOVA)

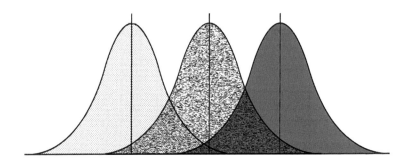

EXPERIMENT: You take samples from three or more groups that are independent and that you think differ by the level of a factor (e.g. dose of a drug, severity of a condition etc.).

STATISTIC: F statistic.

S: S is equal to the sum of the squared differences between the group means and the global mean/the mean of all data. Each squared difference is multiplied by the sample size of each group. S is normalized by its *df1* to make it comparable to s.

df1: The degrees of freedom for S are equal to the number of group means minus 1.

s: Is the sum of the squared deviations of data in each group from their respective meansdivided by *df2*.

df2: The degrees of freedom for s are equal to the number of data minus the number of group means.

This test does not say which mean is different from which. Differences between individual groups can then be tested using Student T statistics.

TESTING EFFECTS OF TWO FACTORS
(TWO-WAY ANOVA)

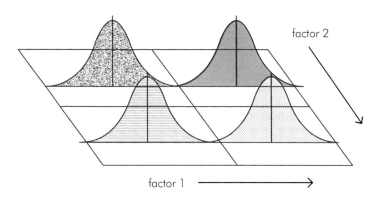

factor 2

factor 1 ⟶

EXPERIMENT: You wish to evaluate the effects of two interventions (or factors). For example two different drugs. You then sample four independent groups. One group is the control group (or placebo) where no intervention is applied. Then you sample two more groups, each one with one intervention only. Finally you sample a fourth group, one where both interventions are applied. This group is important because it provides information on whether the two interventions interact.

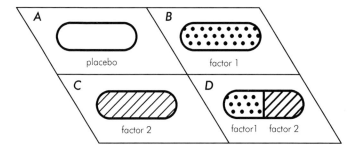

This design helps to test if there is a mean change due to either **factor 1** or **factor 2**. More importantly, it helps to test whether the two factors interact e.g. whether the result of the presence of both factors results in an effect equal to the sum of the measured effects of factor1 and factor 2. For example, two drugs used at the same time may inhibit each other or, alternatively, one can amplify the effect of the other. In the scheme above, cell A denotes the control (placebo) cell, cell B indicates the cell with **factor 1** only, cell C indicates application of **factor 2** only, cell D indicates application of **factor 1** and **factor 2**.

Now, there are three different tests one can do. Two tests independently check whetherthe effect of factor 1 or factor 2 are significant. These are called Main Factors. The third one tests whether the two factors interact.

TESTING x FACTOR 1

STATISTIC: F statistic.

S: S is equal to the sum of the squared differences between the mean of groups A+C (where factor 1 is 0) and the mean of groups B+D (where factor 1 is active) and the global mean/the mean of all data. Each squared difference is multiplied by the sample size of each group. This is divided by *df1* to make it comparable to s.

df1: The degrees of freedom for S are equal to the number of group means (two) minus one, hence is 1.

s: Is the sum of the squared deviations of data in each group from their respective meansdivided by *df2*.

df2: The degrees of freedom for s are equal to the number of data minus the number of group means.

TESTING x FACTOR 2

STATISTIC: F statistic.

S: S is equal to the sum of the squared differences between the mean of groups A+B (where factor 2 is 0) and the mean of groups B+D (when factor 2 is active) and the global mean/the mean of all data. Each squared difference is multiplied by the sample size of each group. This is divided by *df1*

df1: The degrees of freedom for S are equal to the number of group means (two) minus one, hence is 1.

s: Is the sum of the squared deviations of data in each group from their respective meansdivided by *df2*.

df2: The degrees of freedom for s are equal to the number of data minus the number of group means.

TESTING for INTERACTION between FACTOR 1 x FACTOR2

STATISTIC: F statistic.

S: S is equal to the sum of the squared differences between the mean of each cell and the respective row, column and the global means. Each of these differences is multiplied by the size of each cell. S is then divided by *df1*.

df1: The degrees of freedom for S are equal to the number of rows minus 1 times the number of columns minus 1.

s: Is the sum of the squared deviations of data in each group from their respective means divided by *df2*.

df2: The degrees of freedom for s are equal to the number of data minus the number of group means.

WITHIN-SUBJECT DESIGNS

So far we have considered only scenarios where interventions are applied to separate group of individuals, say a treatment group and a control group. These are all called between-subjects designs. However there is an alternative approach to experimental design where individuals are their own controls; these are called "within-subject" designs. In these designs a measurement is repeated on the same subject in the controlled state or after an intervention. The sequence of the control/intervention measurement is generally randomized to avoid order effects. Here we review the benefits and disadvantages of the within and between-subjects designs. Consider the scenarios below. You have 8 subjects that are given a treatment. The position of each subject represent the value of the measurement on an arbitrary scale. The treatement changes the value of the measurement by an amount equal to the arrow, hence it moves the subject to a different value on the scale. We consider two different scenarios.

SCENARIO 1 (Large baseline variability):

In this scenario the subjects have very different baseline values as described by them being scattered along the scale. At the same time the effect of the intervention is quite homogeneous as the arrows have more or less the same size. This is the kind of scenario when it is useful to evaluate the effect of the intervention on the same subject. Hence the same subject is measured before and after the intervention and the difference is taken.

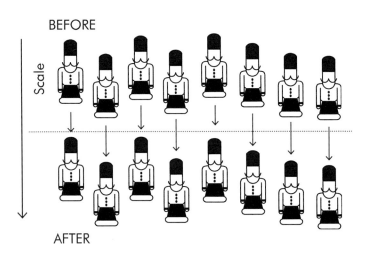

STATISTIC: Student T statistic for paired differences.

Z: Z is equal to the mean of the differences (8 differences in the example).

s: It is the standard deviation of Z.

df: In this case is simply the number of data-points (8 differences) minus 1.

SCENARIO 2 (Low baseline variability):

In this scenario the subjects have very similar baseline values as described by them being leveled. At the same time the effect of the intervention is quite heterogeneous as the arrows have different sizes. This is the kind of scenario when within-subject designs are NOT useful while it is more efficient to evaluate the effect of the intervention on two separate groups. This will provide two independent groups with separate measurements. This may look un-intuitive but note that while in the scenario above we ended up with 8 differences (and 7 degrees of freedom) here we end up with 16 measurements and $16 - 2 = 14$ degrees of freedom.

We can then use the independent groups t-test with 16-2 degrees of freedom (we have two means) hence more power.

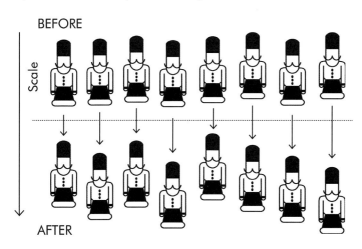

To conclude, within-subject designs are efficient if the effect of the intervention is expected to be homogeneous across subjects but the baseline-values are different. If baseline values across subjects are less variable than the expected effect of the intervention then independent group designs are more efficient.

UNDERSTANDING AND REPORTING THE P-VALUE

This section addresses a very important aspect in the use of statistics, which is summed up by the two questions. What is a p-value? How should I report it?

WHAT IS THE P-VALUE?

The p-value is the number that we obtain by looking at the value of our statistic in our Null Distribution. This "statistic" can be the number of heads (or tails) we obtained from tossing our coin a number of times, or someother statistic, or some other statistic such as a T or an F. Although it looks like a probability, is not a probability as such. A probability can only be obtained by looking at a very large number, possibly infinite, of samples. Generally we only have one. This one sample is not used to characterize the probability distribution of the process we are interested in. Instead we are only interested in knowing how **likely** this sample is to be generated by a purely stochastic process. Hence, the p-value is not a probability but a likelihood, **the likelihood of the statistic being generated by a purely stochastic process**. If this likelihood is small, that is if the p-value is smaller than a threshold (also called **Type I Error** or **Specificity** and usually indicated by the symbol **α**) usually set at 0.05 or 5%, then it is unlikely that the obeservation is generated by a null-distribution.

HOW SHOULD I REPORT IT?

By looking at scientific papers, one can become a bit confused as p-values are reported in two quite different ways.

1. The p-value is reported literally (say my p-value was 0.0001). The value is also used as strength of the evidence, that is the smaller the p-value the strongest the evidence of a non-stochastic cause.

2. The p-value is not reported but what is reported is whether the p-value is less than α or not. If it is less than the chosen value α, that was selected at the step of experimental design and power calculation, then one can be confident that the observed variation is not purely stochastic.

We strongly suggest to use the second approach. This is in-line with what we have described in previous chapters, that is that experimental methodology is aimed at estimating effects and statistical test has one and one only aim, to rule out that the observed phenomenon is due to chance alone.

THE PROBLEM OF MULTIPLE TESTING AND THE BONFERRONI CORRECTION

It happens in data-analysis that one does not perform a single statistical tests but many. There may be a number of reasons. For example:

A. One wishes to use more than one type of measurement (say blood pressure, body temperature, etc.).

B. The measurement has more than one dimension. For example, if one uses a medical imaging technology it may wish to measure changes in different parts of that image (e.g. various parts of the brain, of the heart etc.)

C. In the case of an ANOVA design, one wishes to test the difference across groups.

D. One wishes to divide the population sample in a number of subgroups and measure differences in these sub-groups to control for other differences. Hence one will have to apply the same test a number of times.

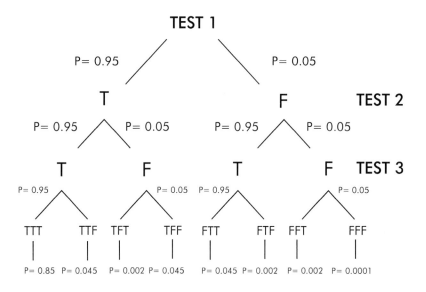

If the Null Hypothesis is true than there is probability much larger than 0.05 that at least one test will be non-null. You can calculate it as the sum of the probability of sequences TTF, TFT and FTT. Equivalently the probability that all tests will be null is not 0.95 but is now only 0.85. In other words, the error rate has increased substantially by the simple repetition of the test.

To correct for the above effect, one has to render the Error Rate more conservative. The easiest method is called Bonferroni correction (from the Italian mathematician Emilio Bonferroni pictured below) and consists in dividing the error rate α by the number of tests performed.

Bonferroni Correction:
$\alpha = \alpha/M$
M= no. of tests

Note however that, by using a more severe Type I error, the power of your test decreases. Hence you will have to accommodate your design and increase the sample size. In other words, measuring more variables does not come free and there is a cost to be paid.

8 LINEAR REGRESSION

So far we have dealt with a simple situation where we wished to measure the effect of an intervention or a factor. For example this could have been a drug, a disease, a particular process etc. We will now call this factor X. We can now imagine that this factor can assume discrete values only and, to start with, only two, either 0 (when it is absent) or 1 (when it is present). Note that in this instance the value of X is just symbolic. We can then call the measurements Y that will be taken in either of the two conditions, that is X=0 and X=1.

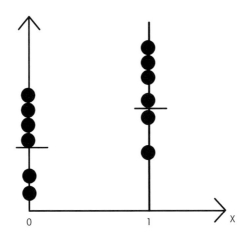

We can represent this graphically. We depict on the X-axis the variable X and we arbitrarily position its two values 0 and 1. We then place on the y-axis our measurements that are real numbers. The measurements taken for the control condition (X=0) are on a perpendicular line to X placed at 0, the measurements taken when the factor was active are placed on the X=1 line.

What we did before, for this kind of data, was to test whether the means of the two groups were different using the Student T test. We can then move on to the second situation considered, that is when factor X can take more than one value. These levels can still be symbolic and consider the severity of a disease, the dose of a drug (still considered qualitatively, say moderate to large) etc. Graphically this will look like the following.

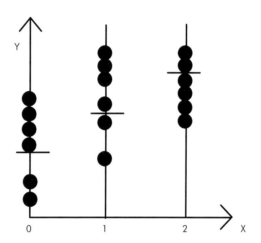

We depict on the X-axis the variable X and we arbitrarily position the three values 0, 1 and 2. We then place on the Y-axis our measurements that are real numbers.

This is the situation that is modeled by the one-factor ANOVA. In the ANOVA at first we tested whether the three means were different and, if of interest one could then use Student T tests to check for mean differences across groups.

We now move to a third case, the case where X can assume values on a continuous scale: we then look at the relationship between X and Y. In this instance, the problem is called regression or, better, linear regression.

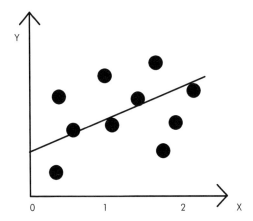

We again depict on the X-axis the values for X that now are real valued numbers. They could be the dose of a drug, the severity scores for a disease or else. We take the measurements Y and we wish to estimate the relationship between X and Y a relationship that, for now, we assume linear.

If before we were concerned on the prediction of the mean change of Y when factor X was present, we are now concerned on how X values predict Y values. As illustrated at the beginning we wish to model Y as explained, in part, as a linear expression of X plus a part, the noise, that will still be unexplained, hence stochastic. X is also called a **covariate**.

While before the data were characterized by a single parameter, the mean, the line that best fit the data is now characterized by two parameters, *a* and *b*.

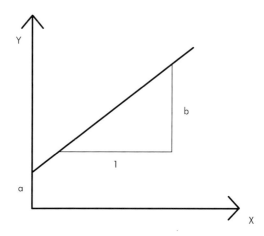

The parameter a is the mean of Y when X=0. Parameter b is the slope and indicates how much Y changes for every unit change in X. The nature of the test now changes as what we wish to know whether the relantionship between X and Y is linear or not. If not then b=0 and the model reduces to a that becomes the mean of the data.

An additional parameter of interest when one looks at linear models is the correlation coefficient, which we indicate by *r*. The correlation *r* is a number between -1 and 1. It is close to one when the relationship is tightly linear and b is positive, close to -1 when the relationship is linear and b is negative, close to 0 when the relationship is not linear.

More importantly r^2 is a quantity of great value as it is equal to the percentage of variability of Y explained by the linear regression. In other words, it says how much of the variability of the data is partitioned by the model. The remaining, which still needs explaining, remains stochastic.

The examples below illustrate cases of increasing linear relationship between X and Y. However note that in the bottom right panel, although a functional relationship between X and Y is clear, the correlation is 0. This is because r measures the linearity of the relation. In this case the relationship is there but is not linear, hence $r = 0$.

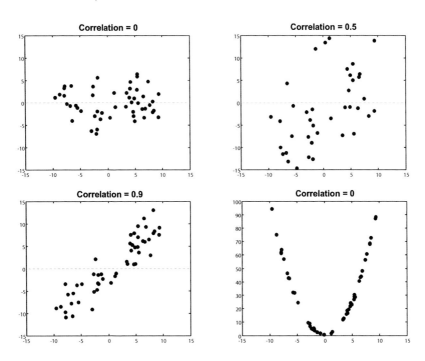

How do we decide whether X and Y are linearly correlated? We use a statistical test obviously. We can go two ways. One is to test whether the parameter b is different from 0. It turns out that if the stochastic component in the data is Gaussian, then the distribution of parameter b is also gaussian and one can calculate its standard error. Hence one can use a Student t-test to check whether the parameter b is different from 0 or not. Note that in this instance the Student t distribution has a number of degress of freedom equal to the number of data minus two. Why two? Because we have used the data to calculate two parameters, a and b. Alternatively one can test whether the correlation coefficient r is different from 0. It turns out that the two tests are equivalent.

9 GENERAL LINEAR MODEL

So far we have expressed the data as either function of a single factor or a single covariate. However the concept can be expanded. The variation of the data can now be seen as either explained by deterministic factors and covariates plus the unexplained/stochastic part. Hence statistical modeling is the art of finding the deterministic variables that explain the data. This way of explaining the data is called the general linear model.

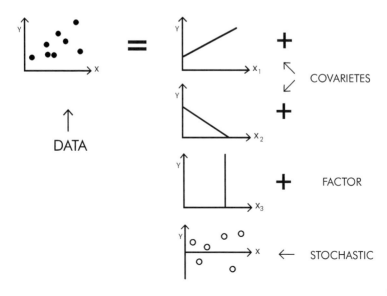

But then how do we decide what covariate or factor explains a significant part of the data?

We introduce the coefficient R^2 which is the equivalent of r^2 for the single linear regression we saw in the previous chapter. R^2 is the percentage of variance in the data explained by the deterministic factors. Theoretically we could add how many factors and covariates we wish as long as R^2 increases. However adding more variables runs the risk of simply chasing noise. So each factor or covariate must add a significant amount to R^2. Alternatively, R^2 is penalized for every deterministic element added.

There are two ways to go about this process. The first is to start using a whole set of factors and covariates that we believe might explain the data.

We then start eliminating the one that explains a smaller percentage of the data variability and we go along eliminating variables until we cannot proceed without eliminating a variable that explains significantly our data.

This method is called backward selection. The other way is to work the opposite process by adding one variable at a time starting with the one the explains most of the variability and stopping when no other variable can explain a significant bit of the data. This is called forward selection. The two processes are not equivalent. The second process is more conservative than the first by which we mean that is more difficult to take in a variable in the model. Indeed the two processes represent two different scenarios in inference.

In the first one we may have previous evidence that these factors and covariates may explain the data so we start the analysis by including them. In the second scenario the previous evidence is lacking so we wish to be more cautious about the inclusion of variables.

ABOUT THE AUTHOR

Federico Turkheimer is professor of Neuroimaging (Analysis and Statistics) at King's College London. He is an electronic engineer by training, holds a PhD in Nuclear Medicine held appointments at the National Institute of Mental Health (Bethesda. USA), at the University of Cambridge and Imperial College London where he was Reader in Mathematical Neuroscience until 2012. He values the tremendous role of quantitative sciences in the formative path of students and in the neurosciences and enjoys teaching Statistics from the basic notions of evidence based decision making to their more sophisticated application to functional brain measures, imaging but also genetic and genomic data.

19189819R00052

Printed in Poland
by Amazon Fulfillment
Poland Sp. z o.o., Wrocław